GW00802465

Strasbourg

ALAN JUDE MOORE

salmonpoetry

Published in 2010 by
Salmon Poetry
Cliffs of Moher, County Clare, Ireland
Website: www.salmonpoetry.com
Email: info@salmonpoetry.com

ISBN 978-1-907056-32-1

Cover photography: *Brian Moore*
Cover design & typesetting: *Siobhán Hutson*
Printed in England by imprint*digital*.net

Salmon Poetry receives financial assistance from the Arts Council

to Alek & Mitya

Acknowledgements

Acknowledgement is due to the editors of the following publications in which a number of these poems have appeared:

Poetry Ireland Review, Cyphers, The Stinging Fly, Moloch, Marks (Ireland); *3:AM Magazine, Mimesis, Iota, The Lantern Review* (UK); *Ping Pong, Moonlit Magazine, the fifteen project, The American Poetry Journal* (USA); *Poetry Salzburg Review, Grasp, The Kakofonie* (Austria, Czech Republic & Germany).

Contents

Exile

from the square you stretch
like marble limbs
into the cold river Arno
wait for the police to move along the bridge

arrest the flower sellers and the pharmacist

pounding petals and grinding tablets
behind the pizzeria

in the archways shelter middle-aged
Englishmen carving up Tuscan hills

like
        slices
                of tripe
                        piled
                                on a plate

movements of statues hardly noticed

the patrons' stiff fingers and thin cut lips
waiting for plans to unfold
for the work of centuries to come about
and turn to flesh from stone

                ★

from the square you stretch like muscles
cut at human angles

s
m
a
ll
neon crosses
s
u
s
p
e
n
d
e
d

in rows of broken fairy lights

heaven is far away

past the porticos

the medicinal smell running through the gutter;

machines for the office face out to the street
three ladies disappear
in the hallway of a church
light expelled – in the dark they walk

when there is love what's left
only death to think of?

★

the sad eyelids
and small mouths
of Irish women
closing by themselves

it could not be you;
your Swedish lips
and arm hair blonde
electrified into stance

no

we are like stones descending
in these metal boxes
riding concrete funnels
we believe
we are getting closer

★

how does a person pass the ovens
walk down the streets of Dante the exile
without feeling the lick of flames
the memory of smoke and bone?

all levels arrive at the centre
all paths twist from the same strait
and here with our hearts and politics
here we congregate

like porcelain horses lashed to the wheel
we scream out for someone
who will take everything away
and make our journey lighter

we skirt along the border
tease ourselves with belief
faced still with the body mechanic
as if for the first time god deserted

and all our machinery somehow
driven by internal electricity

★

the radiogram repair sign sparks to life in the rain

old women moan at old men walking
from tiny autobuses crossing the town

no longer move through the shadow of the Dome
stay close to the river and wait for the wind

to blow them a little further down
into the jaws of the founding mouth

★

the precast faces of stubborn girls
and luminous shapes moving into caves;
you become some kind of brothel interpreter
learning the lines over and over
repeating the rules and praying for silence

the soft footsteps
and plump red lips
grasping for the light

★

located finally
picked up by satellites

    wandering in the centre

the women have wrestled with daring confessions
the priest has given them his hardest look

like you I think they are like you
shaped by absence and history well

along the railway fascists left their slogans
directions for these well oiled engines
the iron road crawling along the spine
of what's left of the empire

leaves are blowing towards the edge
of places where they have gathered
on the platform we wait for the lights to change
and be taken to the Terminal

      ★

dogs are searching in the woods
for the scent of goats and farm birds

lemon trees dip in the rain
and streets unravel from the square

into the plain on the *superstrada*
billboards line the way like headstones;

the empty mouths of soldiers' ghosts
hands bent like copper wire
frozen on the way to Rome
                yet on we go

through the motions
and slow incendiaries

dive down through cloud wrapped in metal

glide   past bodies of water
                    mapped
                            marked
                                    and measured

we wind up on an island drifting like fog
across the forgettable grey cities of the north

Station Road

a river of cloud drowns the beacons
crane lights and petrol signs
float   along   the   street

in alleyways people hold
                    on to the edge of creation

to lowered faces that meet them in the rain

the cadence of coins
                    dropped
in pools of water
                              overhead
the ripple of aeroplanes

lonely horses slip from the side of a stream
the mother's breast rested
          beside fallen telegraph poles

speeding lights congregate
towards lost destinations
draw the coast along the head
rising from the dimmers

the sound of a train loaded down
the mull of electricity
voices bearing on the wires
reaching out for satellites

buzzed through the temporary
shades of darkness across the sky

like ghosts of birds moving
towards the shores of hidden islands

Navigation

these disgraces we carry around are heavy
but we want for nothing
we cannot locate outside of ourselves
deserts cleared of names
mountains without footprints
or water unbroken by propellers

these disgraces we carry around are heavy
yet they have come so far to be with us
to help in our formation
we look for the body without caresses
a type of skin we have not risen against before
we dissolve out of religions

to the chambers of our choice
we disgust ourselves with age
dressed in smoke and flames
become fluid like molten plastic
we cross the world to find places
we must rename navigating the river

to drift out to the ocean

Eden Quay

a flock of birds open out
over Eden Quay
slow movements fading
almost completed

descend through skyline
of scaffold and light
a stack of wings
on the South Bank buildings

driven then over grain store towers
divorced in gauged aluminium beams

one by one accept the race
the form of photographs
the hovering monitor
helicopter blades

newspaper stories
and clouded head
chimneys blinking
across the bay

a flock of birds open out
from Connolly's broken arms
swoop through motorcade
fumes and wails

crash past the tiny turbulence
of glass bank walls
and retro-fit air conditioned excise rooms

the noise of steel
ringing through
Montgomery Street

secret passageways
of dead men buried
beneath ministerial corridors
and financial stations

the loop rings of line ropes
and tram track scars

winding northward
towards rising waters
veering starboard
slide to the east

a stack of wings
slowly fading
aluminium beams

rendered from the city

launched finally out to sea

Maria Rosato

        wore black until the day she died
colour of songs and death
singing and dying consume us

stood by heavy curtains
half-drawn attending to the light
as if it depended on our presence

to move through the room
slide over wood
cast itself around
shapes of metal and porcelain

cling to the side of whiskey glasses
dance for a moment in the droplets

and exit amber against the wall

        dressed in black with children
travel back over barren places
eaten out of mountains
like an empire of hunger

rising through the ranks
of the merchants and the saved
no more fish knives and moustaches

untidy belts or wide lapels
no more lives lost
unwrapped and uncoddled

we are old foreigners
lasted this time
against the glass
the shutter
and clicks

time now in the counting and the prayers
to arrange the shades against each other

to rummage through memories
of funerals and music

Mrs. Colohan

I am piecing together a map
of unknown relatives
and others encountered
when I could not tell
what they might have meant to me
or I to them

except hands held briefly
and dark smiles in hospital yards
half stolen from photographs
ushered back into the car
down long driveways home

filing sweets and change
by weight in suitable pockets

     ★

I am piecing the map together
the good and the bad
to fill the gaps left
by language bitterness and death
stretched by silence

I am not sure what you can tell me
I am almost unknown
and getting older

     ★

I pinpoint past lines drawn
across the city like a latticed tart
again and again
back and forth

we have fallen in
risen up and out of it
laid down beneath
this heap of red brick and gougers

often I felt it would collapse
or melt into the silt
and say we never existed

without this

two strands connected
where water meets the road
and you might have considered
men across the river
asking questions of engines
and the mechanics of trade

waiting boats and motorcars
bicycles and trams

to be bought or to be sold
honesty / dishonesty

the stinging grease and frying fat
speckled counter in Gloucester Street

wounded hands salted
and out into the night-town

these are the beginnings
the formation scars

waves well before breaking

stone steps to the river

Castel Sant' Angelo

looking down on us   the pockmarked
abandoned spaces of chariots and angels

       the heavy locked gates left behind
by emperors and popes

all the time changes wrestled from the past
drag us up from mudland bog and marsh

along the river   like robes flowing
gathering in those around it

small waves and currents run
from the port to the colonies and back again

the ghosts of well paid mourners
skip across the slabs
towards girls hiding out
in the brothels of Trastevere

home they walk   sullen and slow
on chipped pavements; the stench of crucifixions

mixed with baking bread   fish slapped
across the marble   dead eyes removed

home they walk

through the dipping lights running across the ruins
down Napoleonic paths leading to the circus
by the gladiator temples and small boarding houses
the women in their shreds hanging from lampposts

left and right the old men benched and stationary
scooter boys and parlour girls waiting for instruction
hands in mouth   beneath the maps of the world
the standard bearer's empty perch

Strasbourg

in the centre
we are drifting
from place to place

if the lights stay on
we will open the door
and call it home

although
there are no photographs
of anyone from the past

it's not easy
to remember everything
that has been carried with you

we travel out of years
towards isolated shapes
suspended from the ceiling

and streets eaten
by the tramline
lost imagined names

in the dark
your dealings
are done by touch

run your hands
along the wall
of the old abattoir

until you come to something
and the Arab woman crying
in the launderette

recognised the sound of your footsteps
"Boots", she said
"The solid sounding boots of Europeans"

Drift

there is no language now
no nationhood taking up space between us
we have seen everyone
come and go

like small fires in the distance

we have no confessions to make
wait in the laneways
organise ourselves in front of the door
and work on excuses

on the side of passing buses
there are slogans that can be used

and on the funny pages
we are deep in the vernacular
of borderless zones
consumed by passing over

directed through the radio waves
we no longer touch each other
we engage like drifting ash
disappears on the skin

we are rising against the mountain
picking up speed tail lights fade
we have no indicators
no blazing trail where we have been

Concrete

I.

The invention of concrete was I imagine
greeted with dismay by slaves:
the advance of their master's industry
towards a greater state – indentured,
they found new formulas simply created
structures more quickly than before.

We have seen it grow around us,
raised alongside it; our histories newly shaped,
angles accommodated, more moulded
now by metal beams and heavy blocks.
The invention of slaves was I imagine
greeted with satisfaction by masters of industry.

They found structures created more quickly
than before and towards a greater state
we are all indentured – newly shaped,
more moulded, new formulas simply created;
less than science to tell us what to buy
and less than gods to make us believe.

II.

At Ephesus – Greek, Roman and Turkish ruin
– people wait for transport to a house
where the virgin slept. Scurrying along,
the small French nuns pass Slavic tourists
no-one understands. We have learnt to speak
fractions of each other's language.

These other sounds and eastern rites,
the full four pointed blessing and meaningful
genuflection – these are the serious Christians.
I imagine on leaving the house of Mary,
the small French nuns might talk about
the Russian woman exchanging dollars for holy water

while they crush their breadcrumbs to feed the birds
in a garden outside Marseilles. Streets filled
with Baltic girls walking against the walls.
A sort of integration this – kief smoke rolling
through the rooms with boarded windows
and the Slavic tourists no-one understands.

III.

Soon we have drifted past Piraeus
and past the port of Ostia.
We have sat without a sound
behind the walls of the basilica
and contemplated our next move.

From concrete steps we jump
out to surf the ether past Pantheon and palazzo;
these paving slabs,
these arches,
these remnants of communication

left behind.
Faint footprints
drying out in the sun.

And though the revolutions that follow us
are far from perfect, strained more
than formed by human relations,
without these buildings –
these well sprung structures
and concentrations
– would we cable our thoughts
across the sky,

understand there are languages
we do not know.

Attendant

I am waiting here for the running of the bulls
by the broken chassis and humming bird voices
the tears of candles melting from the balcony
and the perfume of burning funeral flowers

I am waiting here for the turning of the tides
by the foundation walls and cracked Grecian tiles
the fundamental noises deep beneath the oceans
dead gulls pulled down strangled shores

I am waiting here for trumpet players
to go passing by in golden caskets
for the flaming wheels and dancing girls
feathers waving in concentric circles

I am waiting here for the revolution
from deep in the mud of our hearts' surrounds
the pulses and shudders of the final moments
the new edge of love the razor waves

I am waiting here for Venetian vases
expectant ashes and the last exploration
the citizens and me go dragging our heels
laying down our markers on sinking ground

Estuary

the sky moves
fractured over scaffolds

past despondent animals
cowering against each other

the sparrows also beg for love
and are swept along the stars

bands of scattered insects
rest on mountains of dust

the first words we said
will shortly be forgotten

the swans have landed
back at the estuary

weary and clouded
they commute to each other

our glances are distant
with no wings to carry them

we will not see ourselves here again

Pipeline

when you step out to the balcony
suspended on the edge of the 15th floor
you reach into the air
as if you could touch it
walk across it like it was some sort of cosmos
mapped out and made familiar

and the information she held
about particles of human beings
disappearing in the embrace of another
or in absolute natural laws

you think of this then no
at this level
you no longer need oxygen
you can reach out and touch
the tail end of comets
drawing back flames to answer her questions
on the physics of things

resting on the edge of the 15th floor
feel the heat of the municipality
          beneath you
the steam vents and metro stations

reaching out to grasp the air
dreams balanced on hidden wires;
all these pipelines and connections
have led us to an island

Dark Green Water

this dark green water
dulled by rain clouds
hung over rusted
barn buildings and outhouses

corrugated shelters
barely standing
by rested rolling stock
and motorway plumage

cable
       lines
              broken

pieces of tile and porcelain
scattered on the tarmac
in heaps behind the depot
will be washed away

into effluent and leaves
become ancient someday
buried in the groundswell
fingerprints erased

         through units of foliage
flow slightly towards the road
between cattle batches
and cellular masts

deep behind the fields
bells ring   hopefuls
hobble up and down
stone streets and the small
city walls

seeds to be sown

tired pools of nightmare
reflect the spectrum
caught on spare branches
air and space fought for

every evening

      ★

substation warning lights
dip in the distance
vast all our carbon remains
breathing in time

with the carriage sway

track clicks our measure
light flickers in darkness
final actions boxed objects
dissolve in due course

outlines

        hair
        tooth
        and
        nail

but we
do not own this
we are not planters

we are transit
from one place to the next

aiming our greetings
and appointments

at satellites
and outposts

at the end of imagination

Northern Line

       small swells pass the bulwark
white tipped sheets on the dark and glisten
sleepers quiet behind northern hills
and creatures swallowed in black estuaries

that slip between the land and sea;
rock wall crumbled and parked car lights
break the vacuum between platforms
still occupied with your lifeless work

pass over the mouths of rivers maybe
suicide bridges and young lovers cradled
vinyl seats in the corner of a field   no harbour left
they want each other to come and go

like boats in a line across these empty islands
beams of light severed in the darkness

```
       s
       p
       i
       k
       e


       n p
       e o
       e i
       d n
       l t
       e


       s c s
       t r k
       a e y
       i e w
       n p a
       s i r
         n d
         g


       c a m w
       o d a a
       m d g n
       f i i d
       o c c
       r t
       t s


       s h p e o
       a e a n b
       c a n v j
       r r a i e
       e t c a c
       d   e b t
           a l
           ; e
```

waving in the wind

Footprints

resting against the remains of the mist
standing out in gulf stream winds

telephone connections masted
roped through the sky for the last time

voices die and the parts inside
begin to disintegrate

pounded down by ham-fisted prayers
pricked by needle faith

there are more than you
searching for saviours

romantic locomotives
easing from the station

and heading out to the meadow –
resting against the remains of the mist

in the space between darkness and light

looking for footprints

Platform

dogs are crying in the distance
somewhere a type of cruelty is taking place

drowning in the noise of cellular conversations
and commuter trains   burnt out cars

on the disused racetrack near the station
in half a field something grows – the other half is
waiting

they are building new platforms to gather us here
placed in a line the sequence of desires

growing the business of grouping together
zeroes and ones transmit communion

sparrows fall from lamplight like flowers
through shallow barking   the echo of metal

Westland Row

we wait here talking
about the architecture of stations

the little dead pigeons
the proclamations

the beam of light drawn
from the clock face down

the glint of aluminium
sparking at your feet

the dust that has not settled yet
floating between us

Region

behind you leave
the city
the tramway

and paving stones

for horse tracks
and agriculture

still standing turret
full of holes

yellow signs
line the road
with bends

breaks

and cattle passes

the sky is moving slow
from cloud to cloud

we will make something of them yet

training past
rotting gates
and culverts

burrows and mechanical carcasses

blackened in the ditch
waiting
for the hammer

waiting
for the magnet

the swinging light
of the wrecking yard

covered furrows
growth restricted
red rooftops

and rusted tractors
pulling themselves through the muck

like slow ponies
or drunken boys

who forget which way they're going

        say to sing songs
about how it was

say to sing songs
about how it's been

sing sing

the dream

is nowhere to be seen

Ship Street

the castle sits on top
of streams and remains
buried deep in the solid
tracts of all that time
passed since founding

since walls formed
over forgotten gold and silver
running beneath us
in underground seams
another thing undiscovered

like the bore holes
and well shafts silted over
half driven into the world
our small communications
measured in torsion

our paw prints marked
on iron railings and steps
straightened up on exit
tunnels left to fold themselves
back into the earth

Mr. Monck

16 Earlsfort Terrace,
Dublin 2

Here Mr. Monck first made
electrical measurement of starlight,
around the corner from the synagogue
and all the ancient gauging of God.

So we carry on:
to measure the pressure
of effervescence,
the weight of joy
on some,
the length of sadness,
the depth of sin,
the carbons and proteins that hold us together.

Down long dark lines
of cobble and leaves,
it finally arrived; on Adelaide Road
I hear the hoofing

of ladies and gentlemen
who still have miles to go.

Threshold

coming through the swinging doors
holding each other then letting go

to imagine a movement that leads somewhere
and drag our heels across the platform

to the corners of trains and feeder buses
time measured by the drift of cells

the noise of aeroplanes
the frequency of railways

faces lost in backrooms of bars
telephone numbers
on torn ends of photographs

     Nothing to report:
Easter on the way
we are not yet regenerated

coming through the swinging doors
standing on the threshold

               then letting go

Spire #2

bullet holes finger width wide
we are not the first ones running from the river

in silence Black Marias
shift around the corner

there are worlds in the wings coming to a standstill

fingers tracing prints across telephone keys
hands   almost   touching

       in the first week of January lights still shine
on the Ministry Christmas tree

the road is lit up like a dirty stream
of Chinese lanterns bobbing in the rain

and your footprints lead back
to a pool of water on Talbot Street
beneath bridge # 3-7-6

you smoked a cigarette in another language
at TERMINUS 27

if only each morning would start with something new;
better a woman than religion   in the end

each morning
people fall
against the pavement

remind themselves to communicate

in deeper and more definite ways

Breath Amended

a gull wandered off its course

unmeasured depths of water
missing in the expanse of cartography

the sound of ships listing against the night
sunken voices fading to the distance

wasted sheets of paper
unanswered mothers' prayers

the lips of other lovers curled with excitement
the worn open thighs lost in deception

her centrifugal force a point of communion

the noise of waves
                     from the beach
      in the darkness
               the lights on the island

the restoration of a timepiece to proper time

       the deep tone of breath amended
the flicker of medical screens

measuring the progress of distance between us

Midland

there is no difference between here and there
except the presence of hills in the distance
and sheep waiting in the corner of a field
to be shorn or butchered; something of use
will come of them

clouds leave wounds open over the road
sunlight seeps through the rain glass
falling on graves in churchyards
names worn down by years of weather;
what comes of us

ghosts waiting on the bend
pictures of heavy handed men
stripped of nature wandering hard shoulders
between Carlow and Kilkenny

dressed in badly cut suits
and rubber soled shoes
the swollen cock
in the off-colour jokes of country women

Antelope

scouting the tiny creases of your mouth
for a space to write my name
I come undone by the arch of your back
the victory applause between your legs

your body is a broken silence
far across the morning   words
fall from the claws of hungry doves
and your heart spreads like antelope

while I'm hidden in the bushes
searching for a new forensics
lost beneath initials and thumbprints
the distractions passed off as love

Beside Caravaggio's *"The Taking of Christ"*

The woman leaning on a doorway, descending into art herself.
Slight veils suspended between them.
Pinned to the stars as if waiting for something
like the leaves changing in October, then to reveal
her world to his; the end of summer broken on the rooftops
and the sky a burning city.

Leaning on a doorway, bending towards the eyes
of her picture Christ: both of them captured by unnatural light.
Her longing for a devastated saviour,
suspended on the wall,

hanging
forever
between us.

Commute # 1

rats run under the track
the tracks are rat riddled
we travel on skeleton trains
carting our bones over the river
like cells in blood pumped
around the body; falling leaves
and creaking voiced stations
wait for us

the shopping bags and boys
in nylon suits take up space
left by women of a certain age
encased in proteins and immunitas
wrapped in hope against decay
the throwaway brides fancying
fast affairs in warmer places;
dead flowers in October streams

in Polish the bank advertisement
is the same as the native –
only words have been reshaped
as if all language works one way
discrepancies eradicated
by keen interest rates or photographs
of a telephonist smiling
back through the grubby window

by the shaking of hands
the secrecy of backrooms
and done deals of dirty governments;
the rats run under the track
the tracks are rat riddled
we rattle through on skeleton trains
wait for autumn leaves to fall
for some sign of grace

X & Y

the earth is flat
territories stretched
across canvas maps

no circum needed
all the journeys we take
tracked on the X & Y

the earth is flat
gated by the godly
from the universe outside

all we need to know
marked on the axis
or scripted in a bible

the earth is flat
pounded down our throats
filtered and smoothly run

a Ford Motor Corporation
          production line
lives reasoned out
in dollar signs and oil

fractions of security
payments laid away
made down on beauty

the earth is flat
and there is nothing
to be done

only a monkey
would not believe
in the shape of things

and this is the reason
this is the reason
the reason is

National

flags wave on the precipice
lead down to the sound
of horns and harps

unknown songs
dictate the pace
heavy boots
thumping slabs in time

flags wave on the precipice
music plays
from deep
historic drains

how little we know of these others
these patriots using our names

speaking of indivisibility
from out on the other side

Rotunda

you not yet formed
born or cut into the fray

you do not know
this falling down rotunda

these walls collapsing into dirt
the chance we make it to the end

standing on two good legs even
sitting up in a decent position

on this sphere rattling
around like a raffle ball

in its small tombola drum

        ★

you not yet dead
withered or thrown into the dust

you cannot know
what waits beyond the insects

the quicklime and the worms
save for guesswork

various and patched up;
our trajectory is a simple one

keep the feet moving
around the axis

until we reach the end

*

you not yet decided
smoking your cigar

in the visitors lounge
(to mask the smell of cleaning fluid

and old latex gloves
that have shoved up God knows what

– that word again those clucking nuns
mutter by rota prayers

for the dead and nearly dead)
you read in the paper

invest in strong bottom coffins

*

you still in this place
waiting for lines to fade

and shapes to move through the distance
into space

have been mistaken
each thing can be replaced;

thick plastic doors
do not shudder in the wind

they snap closed as one goes out
and another goes in

crack and snap all night

*

Record

we have recorded ourselves
and are no longer here
occupants of other rooms
alone hearing voices
heartbeats
through stethoscopes
pressed against the wall
hardly respond astronauts
spin through debris
televisions hum
from the floor below
footsteps
swinging
broken
doors

remember where you are

put it down to memory

tricks that play

repeatedly

Magione Umbria

raindrops on the dog-dish
like Japanese bells

some absence signalled
by these foreign tones

footprints on the slope
marked
and lightly washed away

melancholy canines
rest beneath persimmon

then take back to tracing
truffles

or some other recorded item

Terminal

cold glass lenses
watch over the room
sit in the terminal
waiting for connections

> *it's been years of course*
> *and we are nowhere*
> *nearer to the truth*

when one stands up
and walks away
one unfolds a paper
and takes his place

> *before I call you again*
> *I am waiting*
> *until we both disappear*

secret dark surveillance
bodies lined up
against the breezeblock
clippings of other lives

> *tears dried you will explore*
> *losing fake toenails*
> *in unknown Spanish rooms*

small black screens
switch slowly into night
like sunflowers ordered
to turn to stone and sleep

> *or maybe in time*
> *paint yourself from memory*
> *no camera and no mirrors*

Spire #3

the start of drizzle settles in
across the blocks of living rooms
office space and factory doors

falls dark down garden lanes
voices forced through telephone wire
memory cabled   years before

learning to swim off rain soaked beaches
the curve the wave the slipping under
held aloft clipping foam

and starfish swept
between the grooves
of razor clams

        gulls drift in
        to pick
        the best bits off the dead

water gathers
in the cobblelock
outside red brick buildings

stained brown
never meant to last
eight floors up

functions failing
halfway towers
dissolve in the sky

      today we went over
the old tragedies again

the weaving in
and out of life
the relics of Saint Valentine

people call
from between the cracks
no-one left

here or there
for them to talk to

      rail side they are chaining
two carriages together

passengers begin
to make their way

to the sound of engines and
cheap headphones leaking
music compressed and cleaned

tiny televisions blink in the dark;
6 o'clock

bells are ringing
in the centre
         and at the edge

somewhere there are sirens
somewhere there are prayers

to the machinery of our age
or to brightly painted saints

at 6 o'clock
bells are ringing

passengers begin

            thinking well

to make their way

          this is just the beginning

The Mirror

you have made me something I was not
if you exist   it is not me
but the way I want you
that has become like a ghost
assumed a presence
some image desperate as the fingers
that run through your hair from a distance;
the sweat from our brows drops into the ocean
becomes part of everything
until the shadows of our bodies pass each other
like pearls of steam on a mirror

Sweny | Druggist

p
  i
   r
    o
    u
     e
      t
      t
     e

dome
                  sky riser

weaving over Lemon Street
through the colonnades
past the statue of the queen

harlot perfume breeze
its mangled composition
in the nasals of shop boys
until the vats let out

and someone else
draws you home
along the river
mountains or coast

signal lights break
across the head
tram line clicks
                  the sound
of motorcars and clatter;

guns from one side
                  or the other

the stench
of small explosions
{sulphur
phosphor
nitrates}
        clings

like a kitten ghost
to coat tails floating
out on Lincoln Place
scarred by previous error
fingers yellow tipped
turn recipe pages

pestle crushed tablets
powder bound
in bowls and dishes

waiting   for the loss leader
smart signs
and footfall drivers

bright foil and paper
window dressing   splashed
with sunlight

fades over Easter and afterwards
when it all bleeds dry
when the goods
have been forgotten

book-keeps and tellers
will get started with a passion

     trapped by water
and humps of muck
we hide ourselves
and we grow down

frozen faces
in the photographs

sorrow and destiny
the distance between us

the being
neither one thing
or another

     ★

                                                                 Kathleen

                           sometimes

         I think you must be joking

your tight waistband

           is going to burst

                 and I'll lose my head

                           in all that belly fat

set beneath the Virgin's stare
bronzed young mothers
rest against alabaster walls
and cherry trees in Thomas Square

       broken fruit exploded on the pavement
like scatterings from roulette wheels

perambulators thread burgundy tracks

bronzed young mothers now
rest against alabaster walls

plaster cast Jesus hearts
unhocked pictures of Flemish fields

peasants leaning into the wind;
from small hallways workers leave

bells ringing no god rings
priests soundly sleeping

in dreams expand the numbers
of the stagnant Catholic Dutch

and draped in dark monsignors' cloaks
steal away Saint Valentine bones

take from them all the love there is
drowned in wine and blood and gold

set beneath the virgin's stare
each a cell that spreads itself

                    religiously

Paddy you have been

            singing to the women

                  the same song so long the words

            don't mean a thing to you or them;

                  you run around in circles

            playing with yourself

beating hoops with sticks

      ★

in the country sought
the screeches of the city
the sound of ventilators
noise of brakes
and running of rails
                    underground

the creaking metal staircase
the rising elevator
the chance of explosions
before the evening ends

shot by silence
across hills and fields
the crowing sounds
he never wants to hear again

            here is a different archaeology
the layers of history painted by others

the secret streams
beneath our houses
the bones rising
in huffs of dust

from shoddy graves
and godless pits
our names and theirs
mark these streets

broken in
by boots and wheels
gun butt smack
and horses hooves

cannon fodder
and heavy blades
caught in light
sun umbrellas

walk their children
beneath the shade

★

hobnailed buildings
waiting for the fall
morning functions
standing by the track
murder cries of chimpanzees
we are all the same
when it comes to that
relentless we
repopulate
in twos and threes
small dogs piss
on the marble steps
pram wheels grind
the granite
whistling hymns
and pulling faces
banging instruments
forced copulation
seeding the laneways
the porches and streets
        all of us citizens
jimmying for position
between the dying
and the weeping
brave ourselves
for celebrations;
we do not know
what's coming next

★

each revolving door
each subterranean escalator

terminates
                    you go along
anyway

to the sound of balalaikas
strumming beneath the gates

and join with the exiles
who failed to settle
their heart in any place

while hungry artists serenade the swans
get close enough to break their necks

and paint processions of dead grey birds
to hang in the houses of bankers

they feed each other and go back again
to sing at the edge of the river

the sirens on the rocks
that waved years ago
no longer seem appealing

they sneer at the new ones
who stand around   waiting to be chosen

and fill themselves with dreams
of beauty love and kingdom

dressed in black
old widow mouth

in smoke and headless
treason comes back to haunt us

*

motion sickness
from turning tables

around the bend
to illustrate a point

no medicine for it
competing to be cunning

more country cute hoors
beating each other

on the inside track
around and around again

someday there may be a pill for this

where we have failed so far
some future scientist might succeed

*

one day these wrongs
will set to right
we will balance what's left
on the tapered edge
of our broken little state

and reconstruct
some other vision
not smothered in blood
and propped
on the beaten bones of children

or leave it to the oceans
the swallow of tides
and drag of the moon;
this dark unsutured place
its brutalising done

      ★

pirouette dome sky riser leave
the soap smell of women walking
along the crease of Lemon Street
the soft stains of strawberry beds

grass marked sleeves and buttons torn
quickly lost the liquidity of love
grey reflection in half-shined shoes
small red roses on a handkerchief

      ★

speak to me your eyes are snow
drifting across the poles
your lips are concrete and your body
is streaming to the margins

speak to me: six ribbons of steel
drawn out across the water
hold us up above the platform
dead black horses go slowly home

      ★

out from behind the pigeon wall
here they come
along the shore
all unveiled and naked

the women of Abraham
the women of Christ
the women of Mohammed

they take my hand
and draw me down
into the flesh   down
into the waiting
ground wet and tepid   down

into the sand
hauling back my head
saltwater sky and flapping
up above

      ★

        tramway light

—   sensor   —   movement   — flicker   —

paper peeling
from the travel agent's wall

the frayed carpet in waiting rooms
of hospitals and funeral parlours

in the middle of an overture
the shuffle of shoes
            across the concert hall

      ★

About the Author

ALAN JUDE MOORE is from Dublin. His two previous collections of poetry, *Black State Cars* (2004) & *Lost Republics* (2008), are also published by Salmon Poetry.

He is widely published, in Ireland and abroad, and his fiction has been twice short-listed for the Hennessy Literary Award for New Irish Writing. Translations of his work have been published in Italy, Russia and Turkey. He lives in Dublin.

www.alanjudemoore.com